What's it like to be...
a SPIDER?

Jinny Johnson

illustrated by **Desiderio Sanzi**

W
FRANKLIN WATTS
LONDON • SYDNEY

 An Appleseed Editions book

First published in 2013 by Franklin Watts
338 Euston Road, London NW1 3BH

© 2011 Appleseed Editions

Created by Appleseed Editions Ltd,
Well House, Friars Hill, Guestling,
East Sussex TN35 4ET

Designed and illustrated by Guy Callaby
Edited by Mary-Jane Wilkins

ISBN 978 1 4451 2190 1

Dewey Classification: 595.4'4

A CIP catalogue for this book is available
from the British Library.

Printed in China

Franklin Watts is a division of
Hachette Children's Books,
an Hachette UK company.
www.hachette.co.uk

Contents

A spider is an arachnid, not an insect.

It has four pairs of legs and eight eyes.

So what's it like to be a spider?

I'm a garden spider.

These are not extra legs. I use them to hold my food.

I like to eat insects.

I have a very clever way
of catching them.

I can make
silk thread
inside my body.

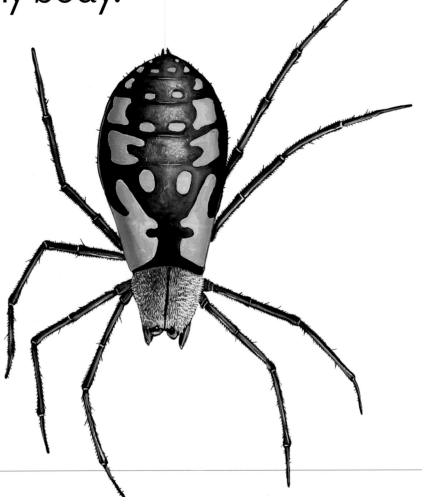

The silk is very strong.

I use it to build traps called webs to catch insects.

Spider silk is stronger than steel wire.

I start by squeezing silk out of little tubes at the end of my body.

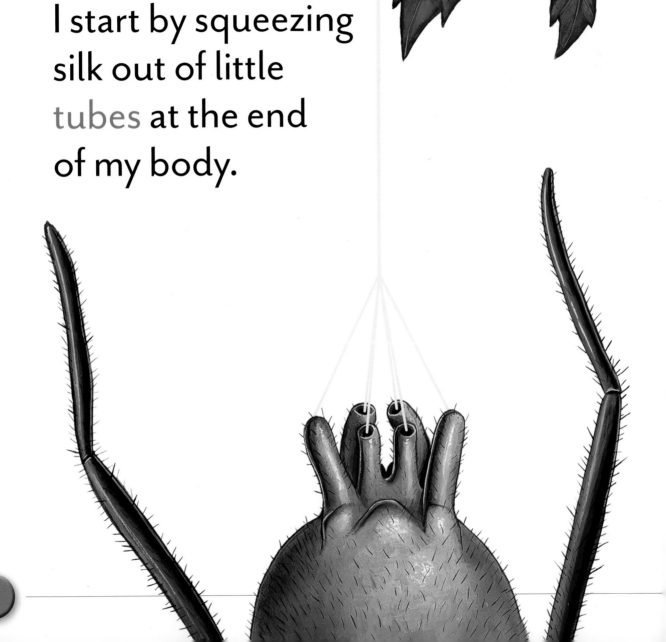

I spin a line between two twigs and I make a frame for my web.

Then I add sticky spirals.

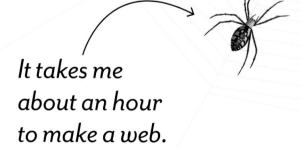

It takes me about an hour to make a web.

My web is hard to see.
Soon a fly bumps into it
and gets caught.

I rush over and bite the fly.

Then I bundle it up with silk until I'm ready to eat.

These are little sticky drops on the silk. They help to trap my prey.

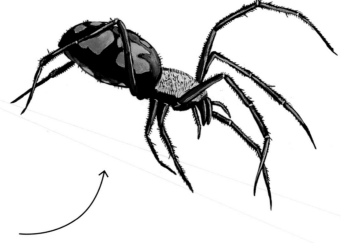

Male spiders are smaller than females.

One day I feel something pulling on the edge of my web. It is not a fly.

It is another spider.

It is a male spider and he wants to mate with me.

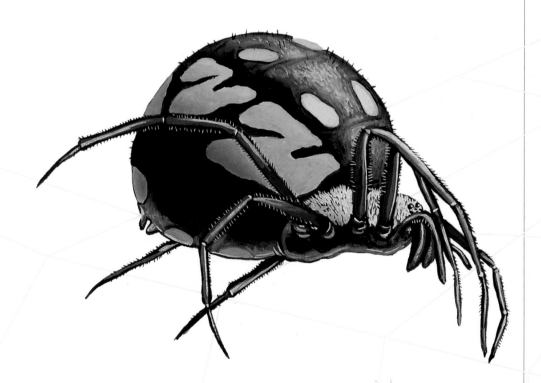

After mating, I lay my eggs.

I wrap them up in silk and put them in a safe place.

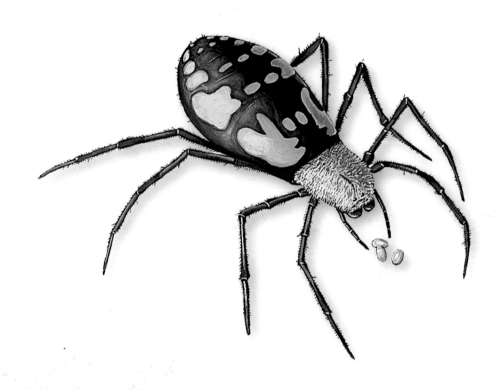

A big garden spider lays up to 1,000 eggs.

That's the last I will see of my young.

 Hello. I'm a baby spider.

I'm called a spiderling
and I have just hatched
out of my egg.

All my brothers and sisters are hatching out too.

Even baby spiders can make silk.

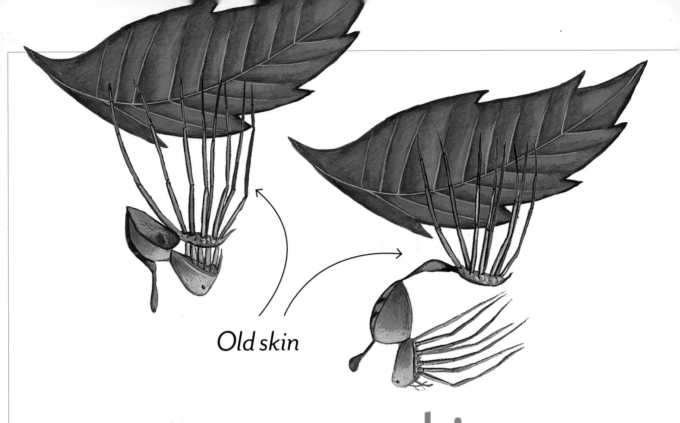

Old skin

As I grow bigger, my skin starts to feel too tight.

My skin splits and I slip out of it. I have a new skin underneath.

I hang from a silk thread for a while and stretch my legs before moving.

Baby spiders shed their skin up to 10 times as they grow.

I need to find a new
home and start catching
some food.

I climb to the top
of a plant and spin
some threads of silk.

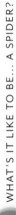
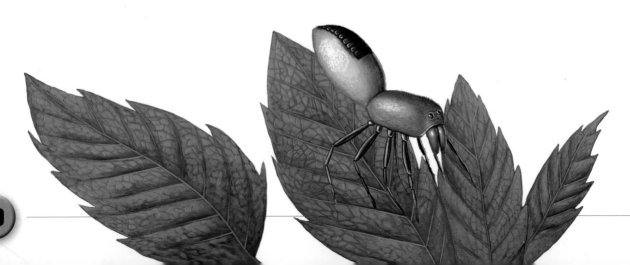

When the wind blows,
it catches the silk and I'm
whisked away to a new home.
Wheeee!

*We call this
ballooning.*

More about spiders

Do all spiders make webs?

No. All spiders make silk, but they don't all make webs. Some use their silk to line their nest burrows. Others make silk traps they hold between their legs to catch insects to eat.

Are spiders dangerous?

Nearly all spiders bite their prey, but very few are dangerous to people. The most dangerous of all spiders is probably the Brazilian wandering spider.

How do spiders make silk?

Silk is made in parts of the spider's body called glands. It comes out from little tubes called spinnerets at the end of the body. The silk is liquid at first and then it hardens.

How many kinds of spiders are there?

There are at least 40,000 kinds of spiders. Biggest is the goliath tarantula. It is bigger than a grown-up's hand and its legs span about 28 cm.

Spider words

arachnid
Spiders are arachnids. An arachnid has a body divided into two parts and four pairs of legs.

insect
An insect is a small animal with three pairs of legs and one or two pairs of wings. A fly is an insect.

mate
Male and female animals mate to produce young.

prey
An animal that is caught and eaten by another animal.

silk
A fine, strong thread spun by spiders.

Spider index

arachnid 3, 23

eggs 14, 15, 16

fly 10, 12

insect 3, 5, 7, 23

legs 3, 4, 22, 23

male spider 12, 13

silk 6, 7, 8, 9, 11, 14, 17, 19, 20, 21, 22, 23

skin 18, 19

web 7, 9, 10, 12, 22